Mirror, Mirror. Who Am I?

By NaTasha Robinson

TO MY DAUGHTER

London

This book is dedicated to you. Thank you so much for inspiring me to be great for you. You and your brother have given me so much life. I vow to do everything in my power to affirm you and love you. To show you how valued you are, everyday. **YOU** are exactly who God created you to be.

Kamaari,I also dedicate this book to you. Never forgot you are fearfully and wonderfully made.

Ryleigh, Raelynn, Courtney, Cyrene, Calvary, Kai, Nazareth and Madison. Repeat after me "*I am Beautiful. I am Smart. I am exactly who God created me to be*" and that you are. TT loves you.

BEAUTIFUL
KIND
SPECIAL
LOVED
PURE
INNOCENT
BLESSED
PROTECTED

I AM GOD'S DAUGHTER

Mirror, Mirror On The Wall.
Who Am I After All?

Mirror, Mirror On The Wall.
You will **NOT** Break,
You Will Not Fall

I am....
Because God Is.....

Unknown

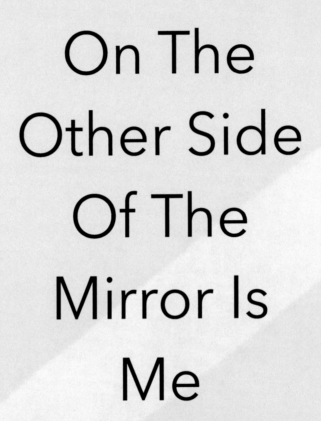

On The Other Side Of The Mirror Is Me

(From The Heart Of A Mother)

"Even if you think nobody sees you, God sees you. And because of that you are worth protecting and worth loving"

Tash Robinson

The Meeting With The Mirror

When you look in the mirror, what do you see? Do you see a beauty beyond ones belief? Do you see a love that exudes from your smile? Sparkles in your eyes, flares in your style. Do you see someone innocent and pure? Do you see someone mysterious and hopeful with grace and allure?

When you meet with the mirror, what does it say? Does it speak positivity into your day? Does your mirror motivate and inspire you, daily? Does it encourage you to become quite the lady? Does it say that you are special, that you're loved and adored? Does it tell you that you were perfectly designed to fly and to soar? Look in the mirror and tell me what it says. It should say that you are amazing, in every single way.

Dear Mirror—

We have come a long way. Do you remember when you searched for your identity in others. You once couldn't find love within yourself, so you settled for a counterfeit version of what you thought love was. When they called you ugly, you believed them. When they called you pretty, you believed them. As if any of it ever mattered to them, it meant everything to you. You were the shadowless girl. Feeling as though you walked this journey through life alone. As if, no one cared and no one was concerned about the girl on the other side of the mirror.

In this lonely world, all you wanted was attention. Making up stories just so someone would be interested in the words you had to say. Feeling worth nothing more than a form of entertainment for all the random people that came your way. But you pressed through girl. Now when you look in the mirror, you don't see the scars from the toxic people you allowed in your life. You don't see the insecurities that ignited every flaw that never even existed . You do not see the words people may say about you.

"Mirror, Mirror. Who Am I?"

Mirror, Who Am I?
Am I the daughter of a God that holds my future in
His hands? Am I the creation of a perfect image,
flawlessly constructed in His likeness? Am I the words
that were spoken over me before I was even born?
Am I the words used to manifest the person looking
back at me? Am I the rib taken from man, to be the
reflection of Him? Am I the vessel, whose purpose is
to bring forth life? Am I to birth generations of
leaders to teach, educate and build kingdoms? Will I
birth leaders that will assist in saving souls and
introducing eternal life to the lost.

There's so much beauty in who I am. There's so
much to be seen that exceeds what the eye can see.
There's so much more I have to offer this world.
More than what the world can even imagine. I am
who I am, and that's exactly who God created me to
be.

10 Things Your Daughter Should Hear From You

1. You are beautiful.

In a world where beauty can be purchased, it's important that you remind your daughter that her features were handcrafted by God to create a perfect image. She needs to understand that her beauty is priceless.

2. I am so proud of you.

"I am so proud of you even for trying. It's not always about the win, sometimes it's about the courage it took to try"

3. If you ever need to talk about anything, I am here.

Some times it can be easy to forget that we once were kids ourselves. Having an open door option for your daughter is extremely important. One day she will experience things that she might not feel comfortable talking to anyone about. She has to know that she can come to you. That should start now.

4. You can do anything you put your mind to.

"You can do all things through Christ, that give you strength" Phill 4:13. It's great to teach your daughter that she can do anything she puts her mind to. It's even better to teach her where that ability comes from.

5. I forgive you

As hopeful as we are that our daughters will never make some of the same mistakes we made, that't not the case. Reality is that it might happen. If they do, forgiveness and mercy is vital. Building a relationship on forgiveness is one of the best way of showing your daughter God's love.

6. You are enough.
"You are enough, just be yourself. Never allow anyone to make you feel that you are anything less than who you are."

7. Thank you!
The words thank you are words of gratitude. By using these words, you are letting your daughter know that you appreciate her.

8. You are beautiful...
"Again, I will tell you that you are beautiful not only from the outside. Your beauty shines brighter from the inside out"

9. It's ok to say no
Some of us was taught that saying NO is a bad word. By telling your daughter that she is free to tell people "NO" you are encouraging her to use her voice and make decisions on her own.

10. I LOVE YOU!
No, it's not good enough for your child to just know that you love her. You have to tell her that you love her and let her know why you love her.

"She is beautiful. Not the typical girl on the TV beautiful, but the kind of beauty that smiles from the inside out. That kind of beauty that sparkles in her eyes when she speaks of her passions. The capibility to make other people smile when she comes around. This kind of beauty can not be displayed on an instagram photo, there's no filter that can convey this kind of beauty. For this kind of beauty was given to her from God and place deep down in her soul. If you're wondering who she is... Well baby girl, she is you."

Tash Robinson

Affirmation

What does it mean to affirm your daughter?

To affirm your daughter is to be the emotional support and encouragement she needs while she is in the process of finding herself.

Why is it important to affirm your daughter?

The lack of affirming your daughter can leave her crippled. Easy to become vulnerable to anyone who is willing to fill in that void.

"Yes, sons (daughters) are a gift from the Lord, the fruit of the womb is a reward." Psalms 127:3

The bible speaks of the children being gifts from the Lord. He doesn't refer to them as property or a possession. He calls them a reward, a prize. It is imperative that we start letting our children know the place they hold in God's eyes. The place in which they were created as a gift to this world. Because of that, we cannot allow our daughters to walk around thinking they are anything less than who God says they are. God created us in His own imagine (Genesis 1:27), but unless she knows that, how can she walk in it?

There will be times in which we don't do certain things because we never saw them. If you know it's the right things to do (whether or not you had the privilege of experiencing it), you are responsible. It doesn't matter if your mother never told you that you were beautiful and special, don't allow that to be the determining factor in giving that to your daughter. Training your child in the way they should means more than introducing them to Jesus. It's more than teaching them manners. Training your child means just that, training your child in ever aspect of their life. Your daughter will be what you speak her to be, not who you see her to be.

Affirmation
mommy excercise

Before your daughter goes to bed (every night), tell her 3 things that God loves about her and ask her 3 things that she loves about herself. By doing this, you are bringing attention to all the positive things about her and forcing her to find those things within herself. As time goes by, you will notice that she starts to say the things she loves about herself are the things you told her that God loves about her. The more you affirm her the more she will love herself and love who God created her to be.

3 THINGS YOU LOVE ABOUT YOURSELF
3 THINGS THAT GOD LOVES ABOUT YOU

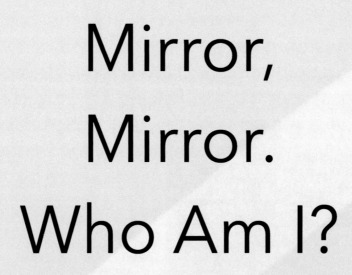

Mirror, Mirror. Who Am I?

A Question For God's Daughters

Inner Beauty

"Rather, it should be that of your inner self, the unfading beauty of a gentle and quiet spirit, which is of great worth in God's sight. For this is the way the holy women of the past who put their hope in God used to adorn themselves."
1 Peter 3:4-5

It's so easy to love the things about us that people can see. If we're told that we are beautiful, we feel beautiful. If we are told that we have pretty hair, we feel like we have pretty hair. That is why it is so important for us to love ourselves from the inside out. Love the parts of yourself that no one loves. The parts of yourself that are so hidden they can go unnoticed. Your sense of humor, your kind heart, your curious mind. Everyone goes through a point in their life when they may not feel the prettiest and when that happens, it's okay. It's okay to have a day when you don't feel so great. When that happens, you look in the mirror and you say, "You are more beautiful than you can even imagine. You are beautiful from the inside out." Even if you don't believe it. Say it until you do. "**I AM BEAUTIFUL. I LOVE ME.**" Do this until you believe it. Once you start to believe it, tell yourself all the things you love about yourself. Tell yourself everything you love about yourself.

You have to learn at young age how much you mean to yourself how precious you are. We live in a world that may have you doubting who you are. Take some time to find out the things that you LOVE the most about yourself. So tell me, what are 3 things you love the most about yourself? And after you tell me 3 things you love about yourself, I will tell you 3 things I love about you.

Inner Beauty
mommy poem

REPEAT AFTER ME

I might not always feel pretty...
I might not always feel cute...
But I know who I am...
I know who I belong too...
My smile is special...
And my personality is too...
I make so many people laugh...
With the funny things I do...
Nothing no ONE can say...
Can make me forget...
Just how much love I give...
And how much love I get.
So excuse me, If my confidence is a bother...
I just know who I belong too...
I just know my Father.
-Amen

Confidence

The word confidence means to be assured in yourself. Knowing you have the knowledge and the ability to do something means you have confidence in yourself. I always *want* you to be confident in yourself. I want you to know that you can do whatever you want to do; that you can do whatever you want to do,whatever you want to be when you grow up. There are no limits to the things that you can do nor the things you can accomplish if you have confidence in yourself.

Your confidence will take you places that your fears will prevent you from going. Confidence will tell YOU to GO when fears are trying to keep you still. When you need it to, confidence will overpower you being nervous.There will come a day when you want to try something new, and the people around you may try to discourage you. Don't let their discouraging words or behaviors derail you from what God has in mind for you.

When all else fails you, your confidence will provide you the sustainable not only to accept, but to endure the hardships you will face in life. Building your confidence starts with having a strong belief in your skills, abilities and who God hand crafted you to be. True confidence revolves around a strong belief and courage in yourself, as well as trust that God predestined you for everything you will face, both good and bad; and the inner workings of who you are have already established what you can do, who you can be and how you can overcome any obstacle.

Confidence *mommy poem*

REPEAT AFTER ME

I can be what I want
I can do what I want
I'm Confident!
I believe in me
I trust in me
I'm Confident!
There's nothing too hard for me
There's nothing too hard for God
I'm Confident!
When they say, "no"
I hear, "yes"
I'm Confident!
When they say, "I can't"
I hear, "I can"
I'm Confident!
Not Confident in my ability
But Confident in God's ability.

Fearfully Made

When God created you, He made you wonderfully and fearfully. That means He made you unique and marvelous. He created you out of a pure, clean heart. Everything about you was perfectly designed in His creation. Everything from your skin tone to your hair textures. Even your fingers, toes, nose and mouth were specifically chosen for you. There is only one you.

You were created by and from a perfect God. There is nothing that God can create or even think of that is not initially made in perfection.

What are some things that make you unique from anyone else?

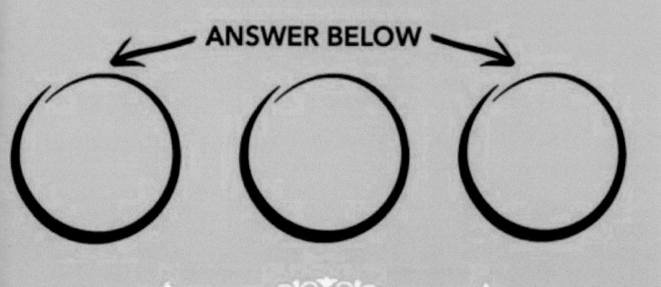

ANSWER BELOW

Fearfully Made
mommy poem

REPEAT AFTER ME

I am *Beautiful*…Yes, I am
I am *Unique*…Yes, I am
I am *Special*…Yes, I am
I am *Loved*…Yes, I am
I am *Cared For*…Yes, I am
I am *Lovely*…Yes, I am
I am *Strong*…Oh, Yes, I am
I am *Empowered*…Yes, I am
I am *Important*…Yes, I am
I am *Fearfully and Wonderfully Made*…Yep! I sure am

God's Promise

The promises of God were designed **JUST FOR YOU**. He wanted you to know, without a shadow of a doubt just how important and special you are in His eyes. He said that He will never leave you, that He will always be there for you. There will be times when you feel alone, just know that He is with you. Even when you don't feel His presence, know He is within a prayer's reach.

REPEAT AFTER ME

Sometimes I feel up
Sometimes I feel down
No matter what, I'm glad You're always there
Sometimes I feel happy
Sometimes I feel sad
No matter what, I'm glad You always care
Sometimes I feel loved
Sometimes I feel alone
No matter what, I'm glad you're everywhere

Being Different *mommy poem*

REPEAT AFTER ME

Yes, I'm different in so many ways
From my smile to the things that I say
From my hair on my head back down to my feet
and everything that's unperfectly perfect about me
Yes, I'm different in more ways than one
Being God's daughter, makes me comparable to none
I don't follow the crowd
The crowd follows me
Just walking in my purpose
and what I'm destined to be
No more fitting in this world, that just isn't me
No more following the group that won't kneel on their knees
No more playing follow the leader, if the leader is not me.
It's time I show I'm different
It's time I show I'm ME
It's time to show the world all that being different has given me.

A Young Ladies' Prayer About GOD-fidence

Dear Heavenly Father,

Thank you for being my inner voice. Thank you for walking me through this thing called life. I have so much confidence in who you are and the God that lives in me. You have encourage me every step of the way, and I pray that you continue to do so. Every day of my life I'm faced with something I'm humanly incapable of handling. But as long as you reside in me, I have all the confidence I need to see the situation through. As easy as it may be to say, it's harder to do. There's not an ounce of doubt in **YOUR** ability, but oftentimes I question myself. Is this something I can handle? Is it too much for little old me to pursue? Can I do it? I know the answers to all of my question. No, this is not something I can handle. Yes, it is too much for me to pursue, alone. No, I cannot do it, alone. And when faced with the reality that I'm nothing without you, I am forced to make an important decision. This decision is to push myself and release myself from the grasp of fear. I can either push until I am no longer capable or I can make myself completely available for you to work within me. I may be young and I may be small, but with your excellence dwelling in me, what can't I do?

Love you forever,

Your Daughter

What is GOD-fidence?
-Godfidence is a type of confidence you have, not in yourself, but in the God in you. The importance of GOD-fidence is pretty simple. Without it, what exactly are you confident about.

Reflections

"You are braver than you believe, stronger than you seem, and smarter than you think"

Christopher Robbins

"Don't ever let someone tell you that you can't do something. Not even me. You got a dream, you have to protect it. When people can't do something themselves, they're going to tell you that you can't do it. You want something, go get it. Period"

-Will Smith
(The Pursuit of Happyness)

"Dipped in chocolate,
bronzed in elegance,
enameled with grace
toasted with beauty"

Dr. Yose Ben-Jochannan

"There's a difference between making a mistake and being a mistake. You are not a mistake."

Sarah Jakes Roberts

"We are beautiful. The kind of beauty you should want most is the hard-to-get kind of beauty that comes from within strength, courage and diginity"

Ruby Dee

"Consider yourself a crayon. You might not be everyone's favorite color, but one day they're going to need you to complete the picture."

Lauryn Hill

Real Love

"Love is patient, love is kind. It does not envy, it does not boast, it is not proud. It does not dishonor others, it is not self-seeking, it is not easily angered, it keeps no record of wrongs. Love does not delight in evil but rejoices with the truth. It always protects, always trusts, always hopes, always perseveres. Love never fails. But where there are prophecies, they will cease; where there are tongues, they will be stilled; where there is knowledge, it will pass away."
1 Corinthians 13:4-8

What the scripture is simply saying is **LOVE** has no conditions. By conditions I mean I love you when you make me happy and when you make me mad. **REAL LOVE** will never fail you. We sometimes fail love, but love in itself can never fail. I love you. Not because I have to, but because I choose to. I made a choice to love you, to be there for you if no one else is there. To love you when the chips are up and when the chips are down. Understanding **LOVE** is so important. Just because I may get disappointed by an action you have done, doesn't mean I love you any less. Love is not measured by the things you do for me, or the things I do for you. Love is just that…. **LOVE, unconditionally.**

If ever you have to question love, just think about God. Think about how God is love. And He loves you so much that he gave His **ONLY** son so that you can live (John 3:16). That's how much you are loved. You mean more than you will ever know. So keep throwing love out there and you will always keep receiving it.

Real Love
mommy poem

I am loved, more than I know
I am loved, from my head to my toe
I am loved, even when I'm right
I am loved, even when I'm wrong
I am loved, happy with joy
I am loved, sad with no hope
If someone tries, to make me doubt
The love I have, I will not pout
I will look and smile, and simply say
This love I have, can't be taken away

"We must lead. Each person must live their lives as a model for others."

Rosa Parks

Building Others

"Therefore encourage one another and build each other up, just as in face you are doing."- 1 Thessalonians 5:11

Our mission and purpose is to build one another up. I'm sure by now you have heard the saying, "sticks and stones may break my bones, but words will never hurt me." This statement is a method that is used to help children cope with bullying. Using this method is detrimental and ultimately does a disservice to them. The pain of a blow from a fist or the sting of a kick often subside quickly; even bruising heals after a period of time, but words can have a long-term impact. Words are powerful, often words are more powerful that most people either imagine or acknowledge. With our words we have the power to destroy, build or in some instances, rebuild others.

Things To Think About...

Do you use your words as a tool to make people feel great about themselves? Or, do you use your words to create pain and destruction in lives of others?

When you see a new girl at school and all of the other girls are bullying her, do you join in, ignore the situation or lend a helping hand? Do you talk about people behind their backs or say nice, uplifting things to their face? Do you keep your negative thoughts to yourself or do you purposely go out of your way to say destructive and hurtful things to people?

Tips For Building Someone Up...

(you should re-write this, because it doesn't talking about building someone upLet's Build Someone up...
The next time you see someone who looks sad and lonely, make an effort to say something nice to them. Find something about them that you like and compliment them on it. Or, simply spark a conversation with them. Simply by offering someone a kind word can make a drastic, lasting difference in a person's life.

And what my mother meant when she said "you can't eat beauty" was that you can't rely on how you look to sustain you. What is fundamentally beautiful is compassion for yourself and those around you. That kind of beauty enflames the heart and enchantes the soul."

Lupita Nyong

When People Say...

When people say, "your nose is big," your response should be, "God created the perfect nose for my perfect face."

When people say, "you're pretty for a brown girl," you should reply, "I'm pretty because I'm pretty."

When people say, "your lips are huge," you should respond with, "yeah they are and they are 100% natural, too."

When people say, "you can't do that," you should simply say, "I can do all things through Christ that gives me strength." Then smile, flip your hair and carry on with your day.

Some people may tell you that if someone says something mean to you, it's best to just walk away. This is a very ineffective tactic. The moment the seed of negativity is planted, it will grow. Negative thoughts have the potential to blossom into uncontrollable low self esteem and doubt. To eliminate this process, it's best to address negative thoughts head on; not by meeting aggression with aggression, but by meeting it with the love of Christ. When all is said is done say the following to yourself... "I am fearfully and wonderfully made. My beauty sees no end. My skin is the complexion God created just for me. There's so much beauty in being me. My lips, my nose, my eyes. All were created for me, with me in mind. I am who I am, and that's exactly who God created me to be."

"You may encounter many defeats but you must not be defeated. In fact, it may be neccessary to encounter the defeats, so you can know who you are. What you can rise from, how you can still come out of it."

Maya Angelou

Credits

Written By:
NaTasha Robinson

Edited By:
Anthony Robinson

Cover Art Designed By:
Vashti Harrison

ROBINSON

FAMILY PUBLISHING CO.

Made in the USA
Middletown, DE
02 July 2020